My Life, God's Masterpiece

His Plans for Your Broken Pieces

Michellita Taylor

Copyright © 2022 by

Michellita Taylor

All rights reserved. No part of this book may be reproduced or transmitted in any form or by any means without written permission from the author.

ISBN (978-1-7375310-0-5)

Disclaimer: Various versions of the bible were utilized in the production of this text. They are listed here as a reference but this list is not definitive: NLT

TABLE OF CONTENTS

Dedication v

Acknowledgment vi

Foreword *by* Lisa McClendon viii

Introduction x

Chapters

1: Made Accurately Suited 1

    My Life 2
    God's Masterpiece 4
    The Pieces are Coming Together 9
    Reflections 11

2: Exemplify Righteousness 13

    My Life 14
    God's Masterpiece 18
    Reflections 27

3: Be a Positive Influence 29

    My Life 30
    God's Masterpiece 34
    Esther 35
    Our Role 37
    Let's Be Real 41
    No, Seriously!! 42
    Love as Needed 43
    Trust His Plan 44

Reflections... 48

4: Earnestly Convey Excellence......................**50**

　　My Life... 51
　　A Perfect God.. 54
　　God's Masterpiece... 56
　　Mother-Daughter Relationship............................. 60
　　Reflections... 67

Conclusion..**69**

　　Now What?.. 70
　　Ending Line... 70

About Michellita..**72**

Dedication

To the men, women, and children who may have lost their way and find it too hard to find their way back, you are not alone. This journey called life leads us to paths unknown to us, but well-known to God. I see you, and God hears you.

Acknowledgment

I remain eternally grateful to my mother, Colette Ann Taylor, for always loving me and for modeling unshakeable faith in the face of adversity. Thank you for fighting for me and reminding me to ever think the best of people. You will forever retain a special place in my heart, and you will never have to doubt my love for you. You are beautiful from the inside out, and I'm proud to be your daughter.

To my father (of blessed memory), Sr. Michael Jerome Taylor: thank you for modeling what a man after God's own heart looked like. You always challenged me to work hard and trust God with everything I had. I cherish the words you wrote me almost 30 years ago: "Michellita, trust me, and doubt not. I desire to do great things in your life, but you must always look up to me and trust me. I will direct you; I will lead you. I will uphold you, saith God, and as you learn to trust me in small things, you'll see me work in those small things, and as you learn to trust me in bigger things, you'll see me work in those bigger things. Trust me!"

I appreciate all my faithful friends for being the shoulders to cry on, my cheerleaders when I almost gave up, my confidence when I was doubtful, my listening ear for my life's dramatic moments, and for demonstrating unconditional love and support when times were tough. I often felt like a hamster on the endless spinning wheel. But with you all, I saw my way out. Thank you.

To my students: thank you for inspiring me and teaching me how to be a better listener and a more patient, understanding human being. Thank you for allowing me to be a part of your lives.

Foreword
by Lisa McClendon

As we live, not only do we learn invaluable lessons, but life becomes our teacher. In exchange for our victories and defeats, we earn wisdom. Lessons are privileges wrapped in opportunities. Therefore, I embrace living life in seasons. Each lesson, in each season, allows us to experience joy, pain, sorrow and in some instances, unbearable grief, which can leave us speechless.

Nevertheless, our broken pieces become masterpieces when we choose the brighter side of our brokenness. This is the place where hope in God abounds— He is our eternal hope.

I have picked mics up and put them down. I've been left and I have walked away. Admittedly, I have been wrong about some people, places, and situations. Nevertheless, I've held the Master's hand as I gathered the debris in my life. What I've learned, is nothing is waisted with God. He refines and repurposes what is left of our trials to create His own masterpieces. However, the growth process requires, patience, accountability and most importantly, transparency with ourselves.

In this profound literary work, Michellita takes readers on a journey to the other side of her brokenness. She masterfully articulates how God not only makes good on His promises, but puts our broken pieces to good use, then places them on display for His glory!

Introduction

Strong! Powerful! Confident! Unstoppable! One that can conquer anything! Do these words sound familiar to you? Would you use these words to describe who you are? Sadly, many would say no. Many of us often view ourselves as less valuable or demonize our true worth. Who we were created to be and how we look are both significant to the purpose of our existence. Yes, how we look is important, but not in the way you are probably thinking. Before you were conceived, God had you in mind. He knew exactly what you would look like, sound like, act like, and He knew exactly what you would do with your life. See, God had a plan even when we didn't. Without question, your very existence was neither a surprise nor a mistake, but an intentional contribution to the creation of God.

You do realize that amongst all the billions of people in this world, there is only one you. Can you believe that? There is absolutely no one on this planet that is just like you. Many of you are probably saying to yourselves, "Thank God! One of me is probably more than enough!" Although the media would like to make you think that you are a replica or copycat of someone else because of your choice of hair, make-up or clothing, at the root of it all, you are one-of-a-kind. And anything that is one-of-a-kind is priceless. A priceless treasure could only have come from someone who himself embodies the essence of worth by His very own worthiness. The Almighty God, Creator of heaven and earth, created you.

So, the question that lingered for years in my head is, WHY? Why would an all-powerful and all-knowing God choose me to be born? I mean, let's be real here. He chose my two parents, and He orchestrated my father's sperm to fertilize my mother's egg that had my name on it, to live on this planet. Why would God do this? As I searched for the answer, I found comfort in knowing that God is very strategic and never makes a mistake. When we take the time to stand and ingest the beauties of the earth, there is no denying that the brilliance of the earth and sky and the spectrum of colors that are displayed are true works of art. In like manner, when we look at mankind and the myriad of colors, shapes, sizes, and sounds that characterize us - and let's not forget about the incredible and complex brain He gave us to be creative and innovative - it's simply beyond natural human comprehension.

Throughout the Bible, God has identified us in many ways, but one noun He uses that resonates in me is the word "masterpiece." Ephesians 2:10 says, *"For we are God's masterpiece. He has created us anew in Christ Jesus to do the good works He planned long ago"* (NLT). This particular verse of scripture here is so powerful because it speaks in one sentence exactly who created us, why we were created, and for what purpose we are to live.

What is a masterpiece? According to Webster's dictionary, the word masterpiece is defined as "a work done with extraordinary skill; especially: a supreme intellectual or artistic achievement."

Aww, I just love the sound of that! It's kind of hard to associate yourself with a work of art, but that is exactly what we are. It is not just about the outer appearance, but the inner workings of our beings as well. We must realize that God is the Master of all creation, and He used us to represent Himself in the flesh, to be glorified upon the earth. As His masterpieces, we are Made Accurately Suited To

Exemplify Righteousness, and be a Positive Influence while Earnestly Conveying Excellence. I pray that this book will serve as an encouragement to you and that you accept the awesome responsibility to walk out your God-given purpose and own your royal title of *God's Masterpiece*. Our purpose only serves us well when we use to serve others.

CHAPTER 1:

Made Accurately Suited

"So God created man in HIS own image, in the image of God created HE him; male and female created HE them."

Gen 1: 27

My Life:

Very few people know this about me, but growing up as a little girl, I was often bullied to the point of mental torture because of my skin color, my size, and because of the way I spoke. You see, I was very, very dark-skinned and skinny. I had very slanted eyes and a gap in between my two front teeth. The tight ponytails my mom would put in my hair did not help at all! (Love you, Mom!) It was hard being a little girl in school, and because of this, I developed a complex about how I looked. Oh, and it didn't help that I was very shy as well. I tried to keep to myself as much as possible, yet I always ended up with a cool core of friends.

As I grew from grade school to middle school, I guess the "ugly girl" stage changed because I started getting complimented on my looks. I then was constantly told that I was a beautiful girl, but I didn't believe it because my foundation for self-confidence was like quicksand. I lacked confidence in myself. Over and over again, I would reject those compliments from people and would not receive them because to me, they were empty words filled with untruths, until one day, a woman pulled me aside. I was about 15-years-old and was picking up my little brother from church. She had just greeted me and said, "Hey, sweetheart. You look so pretty!" Now mind you, I had on a pair of blue jeans, a T-shirt and my hair was in a ponytail. I was tired and rushing and was just ready to go home. My reply to her compliment was a reluctant, "Ok, whatever," followed by a few eye rolls and shoulder shrugs. She told me, "Sweetheart, don't do that. I said I think you're beautiful. Now, I don't know what you see, but what I see is a beautiful girl, and all you should say is thank you." I quickly had to change my attitude, and I politely responded, "Thank you."

When I returned home, I told my mother (who by the way is gorgeous) about these different episodes I had with people, and she told me, "Well, give credit to whom credit is due: To God be the glory!" BOOM! That was the moment things began to change. From that day on, my lessons in identity and self-confidence began. You see, oftentimes, we cannot see what others see in us because we have not come face to face with ourselves! My mother immediately placed the attention on God and not me. This was so powerful because the pressure for being what the world considered pretty or beautiful was not contingent upon my physical appearance. It was solely based on my position in God.

Now, don't get me wrong: this new-found revelation was not a one-and-done episode. Not by far! This was only the beginning. I knew that *"being confident of this very thing, that he which hath begun a good work in you will perform it until the day of Jesus Christ"* (Philippians 1:6), was something I would have to live out each day. So, it took work and, in reality, will continue to be work each day. My perspective about myself began to change, and I could not help but ponder on all the millions of other women and men that had this same challenge. Therefore, my quest in the self- actualization process from God's view began.

God's Masterpiece:

In today's world, we are inundated with so many visual images containing the latest fashion, make-up, styles, brands, and all things SELF! We are often looking for something to improve our appearance and maintain what society considers trendy or the latest "fad." The definition of a fad is "a temporary fashion, notion, manner of conduct, especially one followed enthusiastically by a group" (Dictionary.com). Here, we see that this concept of beauty and acceptance by the world's standards is merely a temporary fixation.

The Bible says that *"Jesus Christ is the same yesterday, and today, and forever"* (Hebrew 13:8). He never changes. Knowing this biblical truth, we can begin to see the connection we have with the nature of God. While realizing that my identity is in Christ, the Son of God, He showed me that like His unchanging nature, so my identity in Him should be as well. He is such a phenomenal, multifaceted, and magnificent God. Because of His grandeur, it takes billions of people to show a glimpse of who He is. We are each a part of the Master Himself: *"so God created man in HIS own image, in the image of God created HE him; male and female created HE them"* (Genesis 1: 27).

It can be hard to believe that each of us carries an attribute of God. No matter how beautiful or unattractive we may think someone else is, we all carry a piece of God. And it doesn't stop there. I really believe that it is a continual cycle. Every baby that is born carries another attribute that God needs the world to see. I cannot help but think that God considers everything when He is deciding who should be born.

Like many others, I am a miracle baby. When my mother was approximately eight months pregnant with me, she had an accident in a grocery store. While walking down one of the aisles, my mother slipped on a wet floor that was not marked with a "Wet Floor" sign. This fall caused her to eventually go into early labor. I was born at eight months, weighing approximately four pounds. You see, the enemy had a plan to kill me before I was even delivered, but God meant it for my good (Genesis 50:20).

Not that God ever needs anything or anyone to prove His power or might, but He uses His creation as vessels to display His glory on earth. There is no one on earth like you. Therefore, no one can do what you do like you can do. The sooner we agree with what God says about us, the sooner we can experience more freedom, more confidence, more courage, and more power to do the work He has already planned for us! Hallelujah!

David said in Psalm 139:13-14, *"I will praise Thee: for I am fearfully and wonderfully made: marvelous are Thy works; and that my soul knoweth right well."*

David knew that he, being God's creation, was fearfully and wonderfully made despite the sin and shortcomings that David often faced. He knew God took His time with him, and he was wonderful in the sight of God. David knew this because he spent time with God and AGREED with what God said about him. When we begin to take our minds off our own natural makeup and begin to look deeper into what God has produced in us, we will praise God more and thank Him for who He is as God alone.

> **For I know the thoughts that I think towards you, saith the Lord, thoughts of peace and not of evil to give you an expected end" Jeremiah 29:11.**

Before we were even born or thought of by our earthly parents, God had a plan for our lives. He knew how we needed to look, what personalities we needed to possess, and what our names were going to be. This spiritual lineage should perpetuate good works, but it often doesn't. We are all to do good works for the Lord. We were not just created for ourselves to take up space and satisfy our flesh. We were created for God's pleasure and His glory, not our own.

*But ye are a **chosen generation**, a royal priesthood, an holy nation, a **peculiar people**; that ye should show forth the praises of him who hath called you out of darkness into his marvelous light"* I Peter 2:9.

I will admit I have had my struggles with this. It's kind of hard to believe. God chose you before you even had a choice to be chosen. Before you could even determine your life's journey, God already knew what you needed to complete the journey. You were preordained, like Paul said in Ephesians, before the foundations of this world. When you came into the family of God, you were instantly set apart from this world and placed into the *"peculiar people"* category. Now that word peculiar means "different." Webster's dictionary defines the word peculiar as "belonging exclusively to one person or group; characteristics of one only; different from the usual or the normal." This definition epitomizes the nature of God. God is in a class of His own; in fact, God is the class! There is only one God, and He calls us peculiar people- characteristics of Him alone.

The Pieces Are Coming Together

This insight is so key, and when it is really owned, the need for comparison will quickly fade. We are all different for a reason. Most people who know me know I love to sing. I started singing at a very young age. Like most budding singers, I would use my hairbrush as a microphone and sing in the mirror, making sure that I looked the part. But when it came time for me to sing in public, I had major stage fright. Remember, I was very shy and had low self-esteem. My view of self was not positive, so I would often compare my gift of singing to that of others and would often think that I wasn't good enough. This limited my ability to grow as a vocalist and hindered my creativity and freedom in this gift.

I can recall a time that my mother (as she often did) shared a wonderful revelation about our gifts. She went on to explain that we were each given specific gifts of melodic sounds. Our unique sounds are intended to connect with specific people at specific times. It's like when you walk by someone, and you smell a fragrance; if it appeals to you, you cannot help but enjoy it or even ask the person wearing it what it is called. In like manner, not everyone may like it, but there are certain individuals who will be drawn to it. God makes no apologies or regrets in giving us special gifts. *"For the gifts and callings of God are without repentance,"* Romans 11:29. So in hindsight, when we don't maximize our gifts fully or neglect the ones we have been given, we are, in essence, saying the gift is insufficient. Oh, how much this hurts God! Remember, He is intentional. We must not look to the left or to the right at what others are doing but keep our faces forward. *"Let thine eyes look right on, and let thine eyelids look straight before thee"* Proverbs 4:25 (KJV).

So, the time spent in comparison has expired! The moments of doubt for your need to exist on earth for such a time as this are over. There is no one like you in all the earth because God designed and created you distinctively and completely. Now, just own it!

Chapter One Reflections:

Give yourself the opportunity to reflect on these chapter highlights and jot down a few areas where you need to accept your position in God.

1. You are not a mistake (Philip 1:6). In what areas have you ever felt like you were a mistake?

_____
_____
_____
_____

2. You are a Masterpiece (Eph. 2:10). Do you believe that you are a masterpiece? Why or Why not?

_____
_____
_____
_____

3. We must agree with who God says we are (Ps. 139:13-14). Do you find it easy or hard to agree with what God says about you? Explain.

_____
_____

4. We are not supposed to fit in (I Peter 2:9). Are there areas in your life where you feel like you have compromised? Write those areas down.

_____

_____

_____

_____

5. We are good enough (Rom. 11:29). Do you feel inadequate to fulfill your purpose in life? Explain.

_____

_____

_____

_____

CHAPTER 2:

Exemplify Righteousness

"I will greatly rejoice in the Lord, my soul shall be joyful in my God; for He hath clothed me with the garments of salvation, he hath covered me with the robe of righteousness....:"

Isaiah 61:10

My Life:

September 24, 2002, is a day that I will never forget for the rest of my life. I was a senior in my final semester of college preparing to receive my undergraduate degree in Communications from the University of North Florida. I was preparing to purchase my first house and thrilled about the direction in which my life was going.

Before I continue, I must mention that I was a daddy's girl. I lived to please my dad. Although he was tough, strict, and scary at times, he was a righteous Man of God. His life was filled with positive and amazing examples of the benefits of financial stewardship, maintaining good relationships with family and friends, and always making time for precious and intentional times with God. As an only girl with three brothers, it was hard, at times, to find my place. I mean, it seemed better for me to just maintain my tomboyish ways, but that was not long-lived. Over time, I knew that I had a special place in my dad's heart, and because of that, I lived to make him proud.

I strived to make A's and B's on my report card and worked hard to obtain any other accolades that would boost my "Proud Daddy" bank of encouragement. Well, my ultimate achievement was quickly approaching. I was to be the first of my siblings to graduate from college, and I was thrilled! I was thrilled to obtain the degree but more thrilled about having my dad there to cheer me on. Oh, the cheers of my dad were amazing! I can recall when I ran for my high school pageant and won! My dad was recording the announcement of the winners, and you could tell he was very nervous because the image on the camera was shaking more and more as they were about to announce the winner. Well, when my name was announced, all one could hear were the cheers of my dad, and all that could be seen was the carpet and ceiling tiles because my dad's hands were everywhere! Now, what could top that? I was about to graduate college. These thoughts rolled through my mind, not knowing my dad would not even be there to see me graduate. After living with a short battle with brain cancer, on September 24, 2002, around midnight, my dad passed away.

It was during this season of major transition in my life that I had to really look within. You see, my Dad was one of those types of men who knew everything, and because he knew everything, we really didn't need to know anything. He was well versed in business and faith. All I knew was that I needed to work hard to make him proud; then life would be good. This thinking was both a pro and a con. I now understand the verse in Isaiah 6:1 perfectly: *"In the year that King Uzziah died, I saw also the Lord sitting upon a throne, high and lifted up and his train filled the temple."* See, it was not until my father died that I really began to see God for myself. In many ways, my view of God in the natural and spiritual was obscure because I used my dad as the gauge for who God was in my life. Oh, how dangerous this is! See, my Dad was not God, but my view of my Dad was right up there with God. I did not realize that until I started approaching God like I approached my Dad. Full of goals, accomplishments, accolades - I thought that's how I exemplify goodness and worthiness to God, but not so. I was absolutely wrong.

The prophet had this problem too: *"But the Lord said unto Samuel, Look not on his countenance, or on the height of his stature; because I have refused him: for the Lord seeth not as man seeth; for man looketh on the outward appearance but the Lord looketh on the heart"* I

Samuel 16:7 (KJV). Through our hearts, purpose and motives are established. You see, although I did all those things to make my dad proud, I had resentment in my heart. Although I made good grades and graduated from college, my heart was not right towards God nor my father when those accomplishments were made. I only did those things to win his approval, an approval that I already had, an approval that I really never needed. While coming to terms with the void of my father in my life, I was forced to challenge my relationship with God. I was still trying to understand how could a righteous and loving God allow death to take my father, a man who wanted to live and dedicated his life to the service of God? I had to accept that God allowed it, and over time God's righteous strength and peace was displayed as well.

Throughout the New Testament, we can recall Jesus' disciples doing amazing things with Jesus. They were with Him when He performed miracles. They experienced His presence and fellowship, but it was not until He returned to Heaven with God the Father that they were released to do greater works: *"Verily, verily, I say unto you, he that believeth on me, the works that I do shall he do also; and greater works than these shall he do; because I GO unto my Father"* John 14:12 (KJV). Jesus had to leave in order for the greater works to be performed. So, I realized in many ways that my father hindered my ability to see God for myself. I often think about what life would be like if my Dad were still here. Some of you may be thinking the same thing. It is a difficult concept to accept at times, but we must believe that God knows us better than we know ourselves. Therefore, He knows what is good and necessary for the fulfillment of our life's purpose.

God's Masterpiece

This masterpiece was fractured and broken. My canvas had holes and rips, but it was a part of the process of becoming who I was created to be. You can probably relate. Just when you think things are beginning to move in the right direction, another stumble or blast from the past halts your forward movement. But don't lose heart. Be encouraged. This journey to righteousness is not one that is taken alone. The root word of righteousness is righteous, which means: "characterized by uprightness or morality; morally right or justifiable."

I believe that at the heart of every man, we want to be right, and we want to do right by people. Very rarely will one hear a person say, "My goal is to be the meanest, most hated person by all. I want to accomplish the highest degree of deceit and immoral deeds ever known to mankind." Nope! Not at the heart of a person. Both negative and positive behaviors are learned and adopted by the influences around us, which means we have the capacity to be conditioned and can make changes to our everyday behaviors, but not without intentionality. Most goals are accomplished or obtained in life because of intentionality.

Take pageants, for instance. I love pageants and have competed in my share. My participation in such programs has made me an avid believer in this type of program, so much so that in 2012, I founded my own scholarship pageant, entitled, *The Miss Charisma Scholarship Pageant* (Jacksonville, Florida). I started this pageant because, as a junior in high school, I competed in my school's pageant and had an amazing experience. I was shocked and thrilled when I won, but more importantly, I grew in confidence. As a result of this experience, I knew this was something I wanted to do for other young women. When I began my teaching career at a Christian high school, the opportunity opened up, and I started the *Miss Potter's House Christian Academy Pageant* or *The Miss PHCA Pageant*.

Through my role as founder and director of the pageant, I developed a program that did not solely focus on obtaining a crown, but one that required the young ladies to come face to face with themselves. This was not easy because this platform exposes our innermost insecurities. Therefore, vulnerabilities will soon begin to surface. We must allow others into that secret place where there is not a "Welcome" sign, but a "Beware," "Stay Away," or "Danger Zone" sign present. It is hard to let someone see the down and dirty side of us, but it is very necessary. It is almost like a person who has a beautiful house. When the owner begins to give a tour of the house, there is one room with the door closed. The owner says, "Oh, we can't go into that room because that's where we keep all the stuff we don't use all the time, and it needs cleaning." Yeah, you know exactly what I'm talking about, right?

God wants to clean out that space in our lives and our hearts. David's life is such a great example of being between the blessing and the curse his entire life. David was called and chosen, but his heart, like so many of ours, was wicked. Even though his ways were initially deceitful, he finally came to a point in his life where he needed help beyond his own ability. He wanted transformation. He desired true and lasting change. David declared in Psalm 51:10, *"Create in me a clean heart, Oh God, and renew the RIGHT spirit within me."* He came to the end of himself, and he knew that something had to change; that "something" was himself.

This change was procedural as was highlighted in four words in the verse above: Create → Clean→ Renew→ Right. First, David petitioned God to change him by making or creating in him a clean heart. The heart David was working with was old, corroded, and atrophied. He was a mess and nearly on life-support. Because of this, he needed God to create within him a new heart. David was specific in the type of heart that he needed because he knew his heart was dirty. This is my second point. He was honest; therefore, he knew the heart needed to be clean.

David dealt with the flesh or natural part of him first. Then he pointed out his spirit. Point number three: He needed his heart to be renewed. His spirit was tired and fatigued. His spirit had not been fed or nurtured because his flesh had wreaked havoc on him. Like us, David needed a refreshing that can only be quenched by the presence of God. Finally, he wanted to be right. We can never be "right" or obtain righteousness apart from God. It is only through the precious blood of Jesus that we can be made right again. And this is a daily process. Each day we should ask the Lord to clean our hearts and renew our spirits. Daily we are faced with challenges and must make decisions about the choices we face. Thus, for each day, we need new strength and new power to be successful.

How about you? Is this the cry of your heart? Have you been trying to change on your own? Well, be of good cheer! Help is not only on the way, but help is here. We must be intentional about wanting to change, and we must be willing to do the work. Oh, and don't forget that PEOPLE ARE COUNTING ON YOU TO DO IT! Yes, YOU! They need to see the masterpiece in you displayed to the world.

We are awesome creations, clothed in glory, and covered with the blood of Jesus. We not only carry the characteristics of God, but we are to show forth in our lives His righteousness or "right-ness." We are representatives of God Himself. We have a responsibility for how we look and what we do. It is too often that we come across some of the most beautiful, attractive, flawless-looking people, and we wonder to ourselves, "I wish I looked like that or had those features." But as soon as that person opens his/her mouth and you hear how she talks, or you observe how she behaves, you then get a different perspective of that person.

Nothing hurts God more than for Him to see His own creation misrepresent Him. It is no different from a parent and a child. If a child misbehaves, people look at the parents and blame them for their child's actions. God is the same. He wants us to exemplify His righteousness and godliness everywhere we go and in everything we do, but we must accept the role and be intentional. *"The **mouth** of a righteous man is a **well of life**..."* Proverbs 10:11. Our communication should be a well-spring of life. People should want to hear us speak because they know that what we are going to say is going to be uplifting and encouraging, not negative and degrading. In other words, even though life gives us a hard time and is most often not fair, our words should weigh more on the positive side than on the negative side. God is the life-giver, and if we are an extension of Him, then we should be the same.

God doesn't make us do anything we are incapable of doing. He has equipped us through His Word to be righteous people, and He never turns His back on us even when we fall short of His righteousness. He loves us and wants us to always be in right standing with Him. I have come to learn that it is not my perfection that God is requiring but my daily and intentional communing with Him, coupled with total surrender to His will for the day. Often, I would find myself striving and working so hard to be perfect and right all the time. My intentions were surely pure, but my method was totally inadequate. Through the flesh, we can never obtain righteousness. Only through total surrender to God can we be found righteous. It's strange to think that we try to please God when only He knows what pleases Him. So how do we discover how to please Him? Like in anything else, we must research, inquire, and dedicate time to acquiring this knowledge. God's word provides us with numerous truths to support His standards for righteousness.

Here are just a few.

- Prov. 21:21- *"He that followeth after righteousness and mercy **findeth life, righteousness, and honor.**"*

- I John 3:7- *"Little children, let no man deceive you: **he that doeth righteousness** is righteous, even as He is righteous."*

- Ps. 37: 21- *"The wicked borroweth, and payeth not again; but the **righteous showeth mercy, and giveth.**"*

- Prov. 3:32 – *"For the forward (disobedient) is abomination to the Lord: **but his secret is with the righteous.**"*

I know that you are thinking that being righteous all the time is so hard and that it is not possible. Yes, this is true. We are not perfect, but the key is a sincere commitment that meets the standards set by God. God sees the true heart of man, and He knows if a person is sincere in his relationship with Him. We must give our all just as God did for us. We need not always make excuses for ourselves as to why we sin or cheat or have stinking thinking. We need to go to our life's manual, the Word of God, and see how we can become overcomers of our obstacles that prevent us from obtaining the righteous position in God. Once we condition our minds to attain righteousness, nothing can prevent God's blessings. Choose a good reputation over great riches, and being held in high esteem is better than silver and gold (Proverbs 22:1). Think about this: Ecclesiastes 7:1 (NLT) says, *"A good reputation is more valuable than costly perfume. And the day you die is better than the day you were born."*

Chapter Two Reflections:

1. We must have the CORRECT VIEW of God (Isaiah 6:1). How do you view God?

_____
_____
_____
_____

2. God already has the RIGHT idea for our lives (Jer. 29:11). Are your ideas for your life the same as God's? If not, how are they different?

_____
_____
_____
_____

3. God wants to use you to do GREAT WORKS (John 14:12). Do you believe your life can help someone else? Explain.

_____
_____

_____

_____

4. We must ask God DAILY to make our spirits RIGHT (Ps. 51:10). How can you develop a habit of asking God for help each day?

_____

_____

_____

_____

5. The pursuit of RIGHTEOUSNESS produces life and a good name (Prov. 21:21). Do you have a good name in the community? How can it be better?

_____

_____

_____

_____

CHAPTER 3:

Be A Positive Influence

"Ye are the salt of the earth; but if the salt have lost his savor, wherewith shall it be salted? It is henceforth good for nothing, but to be cast out, and to be trodden under foot of men.

Ye are the light of the world. A city that is set on a hill cannot be hid."

Matthew 5:13-14

My Life:

In June of 2012, I stepped out on faith and started the *Miss Charisma Scholarship Pageant*. As I stated in the previous chapter, I found pageants to be a tremendous source of help in the area of confidence. Many people still find it hard to believe that I used to be extremely shy as a young (girl and) throughout my high school career. I would cringe each time my teacher would call on me to read a paragraph from a story. I would get butterflies in my stomach and have that nervous quiver in my voice each time I would have to speak in public. Honestly, it still shows up sometimes, but not as bad. Ugh!

When I started competing in pageantry, however, I began to gain more and more confidence and realized that this competition is not too bad. I learned so much about myself and about what I was capable of doing: from speaking clearly and fluently to walking with grace and style. It was awesome! This transformation was so significant that I had to keep it going. My passion to make a difference and be a positive influence was birthed from this experience. It's strange that all of these experiences (good and bad) were a part of God's ultimate plan. Of course, the plan is not always easy to see, but this is the time when we have to just let God be God and do it.

It's amazing when we discover that we have so much faith that goes untapped because of fear. This divisive tendency hinders the amazing experiences God has predestined for us. This is exactly what I did. I had just started graduate school and was in a major season of transition from working as a high school English teacher. It did not seem to make much sense to start a new business or program during a time that seemed so uncertain. There was such a pressing sense of urgency that propelled me to pursue this new endeavor. My journey to the inception of the Miss Charisma Scholarship Pageant began, with no money, no contestants, and a whole lot of fear and favor. I began using what I had and doing what I could do. The lesson in this part of the journey was keeping the mission at the forefront of my mind instead of what I needed to complete the mission. I knew my objective was to make a difference and be that positive influence. The fact that I wanted to give back and allow another girl to experience what I did was fuel enough.

During the pursuit, the masterpiece that God was still constructing had to be tested. The test was thankfully open book and open notes! As the planning for the pageant was underway, we got the contestants, hired the staff, and acquired the venue; then, the day for the event arrived. The hotel coordinator was well aware that this was my first event, and she knew about the challenges that we had along the way. When I showed up to the venue, absolutely nothing was ready. Nothing! The banquet hall had not been cleaned from the night before nor set up for our event that morning.

Needless to say, I was a total mess! I was mad, frustrated, and aggravated. The coordinator for the hotel knew that I was going to be upset and knew how difficult it had been to get this event together so she tried to meet me before I discovered the unfinished room. My personal assistant immediately came to my aid to calm me down and assure me that all would be okay. And, oh, how it was okay! LOL. God totally worked it out for my good. The room was not ready as agreed; I received a total refund for the venue! The venue, in essence, paid me for the event. My goal for this pageant was to award the winner with a minimum $1000 scholarship, and I had not quite reached that goal yet, but this unexpected blessing made the difference. During that episode, I learned there is always an opportunity to have a positive influence on someone. Although I was mad, frustrated, and aggravated with the entire situation, I never let the coordinator know. Her compassion for my mission and desire to make this event a success compelled her to make that decision immediately to cover the expense.

It was through this experience that I learned to just trust God with what He gives me to do. I was reminded of Psalm 37:4: *"Delight yourself in the Lord and he will give you the desires of your heart."* Delight means to "give great pleasure, great satisfaction, or enjoyment; to please highly." When we take joy in someone or something, we get satisfied. Think about that hobby or even loved one that brings you great joy. The feeling that you get from investing time and energy in that thing fuels you to want to do more and more. This is what God desires of us because it is during these times that He begins to download wisdom into our minds and spirits that gives us clear insight for our next steps.

More importantly, this increases our level of confidence to move forward in uncharted territories. The fear of the unknown can literally paralyze us and prevent us from fulfilling our true purpose that is directly tied to helping someone else. You do realize that you weren't simply put on this planet just to take up space, right? I mean, you do know that your life is not to be lived simply to gratify your own flesh? Oh, well, if you did not know, YOU WERE ☺! You are too important to this world and God's master plan to be placed on a shelf or locked in a box.

God's Masterpiece

You can make a difference! You are special in every way! Often, it is so easy for us to esteem others, but it is difficult to build up ourselves. Because of our nature and genetic make-up that has come straight from the mind of God, there is no question that we were made to invoke change and to see it happen. The Bible does not lack in the practical examples of how people did not feel equipped or qualified to make a difference in their countries for one reason or another. One individual that I love to reference that made a major impact on their country was Esther. Let's take a look at her story.

Esther

Esther was an orphan who was sent to be raised by her uncle after her parents died. This is strike one. She had no real family that supported her. During this time, King Xerxes ruled over the kingdoms from India to Ethiopia. King Xerxes' Queen, Vashti, had a feast at the same time as Xerxes. Well during this time, King Xerxes summoned Vashti to come and entertain him and his guests, but she refused. This was a huge No-No. The King's court and nobles then said something should be done to send a message to everyone that when the King orders the wife to appear before him, she is to come. That message was the banishment of Vashti from the palace. Xerxes then began to miss Vashti because he was lonely. The suggestion was then made to find beautiful virgins and decide which would be most pleasing to the king to become his new queen.

Well, Mordecai's family was exiled, but he had a beautiful cousin named Hadassah or Esther, whom he took care of after her parents died. Esther was brought to the king's Harem. She was then assigned maids to begin the beauty treatments. During this time, Esther was forbidden to tell her nationality. For twelve months, the women went through a series of beauty treatments before being brought before the king. When it was Esther's turn to be presented, he was so taken by her, and he loved her more than the others. He decided then that she was to be crowned his queen.

When she was crowned, she still kept her family background and nationality a secret. Mordecai became a palace official because he pleased the king, and the king, in return, wanted to honor him. Haman told the king what he should do for someone who he wanted to honor, secretly thinking that he should be the one receiving this recognition. Meantime, two of the king's eunuchs became mad at King Xerxes and plotted to kill Mordecai. Mordecai told Esther, and Esther told Xerxes. When the story was found to be true, the two plotters were killed. Xerxes then promoted Haman, making him the most powerful official in the empire. Now, this was a major turn of events.

As the story continues, all the king's officials were commanded to bow and show Haman respect, but

Mordecai refused because he was a Jew. Haman found this out and plotted to destroy the Jews because of Mordecai's refusal. Now, this is some serious disdain! Haman went to the king and told him that there was a certain race of people that refused to obey the laws of the king, and they should not live. He recommended a reward of 10,000 sacks of silver be given to the one who reveals those who would not bow, and the king agreed to this decree. Not only did the king agree, but the decree was sent out and made into a law. The decree ordered that all Jews, (men, women, and children) be killed.

When Mordecai heard about the decree, he publicly mourned. Esther found out about the decree and was compelled to tell the King. Unfortunately, Esther was not permitted to go before the king unless she was requested and was also told that she would not escape this decree. In a courageous attempt to save her people, Esther orchestrated a banquet because important decisions were made during feasts. This would provide the perfect opportunity for her to plead her case before the King. So, the king and Haman went to Queen Esther's banquet. King Xerxes asked Esther what she wanted, and she replied that her life and the lives of her people be spared because Haman put out the decree to have the Jews killed. Haman eventually died on the sharpened pole that he built for Mordecai to be impaled on. Esther further requested that her people be saved. Because of her relentless boldness, she and her people were freed, Haman and his sons were killed on the sharpened poll, and the Jewish people were never to be placed under that type of decree again.

Wow! What a story. Here we can reflect on three main lessons that can help us to realize that although we may not feel qualified, God qualifies us.

1. Esther was an orphan, which meant she was downgraded. She did not really have a true identity because she was raised by another family member. Although Esther was qualified by her virginity to be a candidate for Queenship after Vashti was dethroned, she still required the favor of her Uncle to position her to be queen.

2. Haman enacted a decree for the Jews to be killed because Haman was jealous of the favor that Mordecai

had, and Mordecai refused to bow to him like the others.

3. Esther was not only beautiful, but she was bold and courageous. In order to save herself and her people, she had to be smart about how she would make this forbidden request to the king. Not just that, going before the king was not welcomed. She had to be requested to come forward. But despite these apparent roadblocks, she accomplished her goal.

Our Role

After knowing WHO we are and WHY we were created, we should want our lives to be a reflection of God's glory. We should be sharing our new discovery of His manifested glory to others. The beautiful thing about sharing our victories with others is that it strengthens us. When we are stingy or selfish with the good news of what God has done for us, it weakens the power of the story. Even as I write at this moment, I can't help but smile because of the joy I feel in knowing that this book is going to encourage someone. You see, I am already benefiting from telling my story. Our testimony is powerful as

Revelation 12:11 states: *"And they overcame him by the blood of the lamb and by the Word of their testimony and they loved not their lives unto the death."* The "him" in this verse of scripture is referring to the devil or Satan. During this verse, a war was taking place in the heavens with Michael the archangel and Satan. At the end of the fight, the enemy (Satan) was thrown out of Heaven, and they overcame him.

In telling our stories to others, we remind the enemy that we are victorious. It is a domino effect in that when I tell someone my story, I am reminded of my victory, and someone else is encouraged and strengthened. Consequently, that person tells someone else, and he or she is also encouraged. They now have a positive outlook on their present situation. Those who have made the connection and discovery about the lesson learned through the experiences of others have the opportunity to grow. You know those people who smile when you are rude or compliment you when you are upset? Yeah, those are the folks I'm talking about. Being positive comes naturally to them because it has become a daily practice. Yes, we must practice being positive. Like everything else, it takes effort to start a new habit to see real and lasting change. That's how it ought to be, but, yes, it is an intentional decision one must make each and every day. This masterpiece that God has and is creating in us requires one piece at a time. We both are and are becoming His greatest work each and every day.

Let's Be Real

It is no surprise, however, that a person can be on the mountaintop one minute and then down in the valley the next. Feeling depressed, empty, lonely, or unhappy can arrive surreptitiously. We can look on social media, turn on the television or radio, or simply begin a conversation with a friend and be greeted with bad news. More than that, bad news will find us. Can you relate?

In my life, I have experienced severe depression and oppression to the point of suicidal thoughts. Yes, suicide. When I was in middle school, I can recall a time I took a bunch of pills and passed out on the bathroom floor. During that time, I had such low self-esteem because I was daily taunted about my size and skin color. Even having friends did not seem to matter. Within myself, I was so sad and depressed and did not like myself. Unfortunately, there are many that were successful in their suicidal attempts and aren't living to tell their stories like I can. For this, I am so grateful to God. The enemy would want nothing more than for us to be so hard on ourselves and think that our lives aren't important. He feeds us with lies of inadequacy, failure, shame, and defeat. Jesus tells us: *"the thief (the devil) cometh not but for to steal, and to kill and to destroy, but I have come that you might have life and that more abundantly"* John 10:10. We have an advocate, the best there is, to guide and support us in our predestined plan.

No, Seriously!!

In this world, we can never be successful alone. There are so many that suffer every day in silence from low self-esteem and are faced with the decision to just give up. But they do not have to. Why, you ask? Because they have YOU! Embracing the love of God by embracing love for ourselves, both internally and externally requires intentional attention to being whole and complete in God.

Our completeness in God is likened to a symphony of musical arrangements and instrumentals, meticulously constructed to produce a specific harmony. We should be the instruments resounding in the ears of people to enjoy life and love themselves. One of the secrets of lasting joy is the joy we have enabled others to experience through intentional sacrifice, acts of kindness, and compassion. That is the secret to true joy and happiness, and there are endless ways that we can do this. It may just be by giving an encouraging word or telling someone that her hair looks nice. The smallest compliment or comments can make someone's day better. Love is the most powerful display of selflessness one can demonstrate. God is love, and if we are made in His image and likeness, we should show love also. Matthew 15:12 states: *"This is my commandment, that you love one another as I have loved you."* But how do we know how God loves us? We must learn and purpose to be intentional.

Love as Needed

Believe it or not, loving people the way we want to love them is biased love. Loving people the way God loves them is complete. His love is unconditional, no strings attached. This is something we should want to do. Knowing who we are and whose we are makes loving people a less daunting task. Many people today have trouble loving others because of past hurts or relationships. You may have exhausted love and passion for a business or a ministry, and in return, you were wounded, causing you to withhold loving again. Be encouraged. Remember, nothing happens by accident. Each and every stumbling block that we have had to overcome or platform we have been awarded to stand on was in the full plan of God. It is just up to us to see God's goodness in it.

Trust His Plan

Initially, when I went to college, my plan was to study broadcast journalism, but at that time, I did not want to move or start over in another city. I was fearful, so I changed my major to Public Relations. Well, that did not come out well, either. My father passed away three months before my graduation, and following that, I took a job that had promises of my having the ability to make a lot of money. Ha Ha! What seemed too good to be true most certainly was.

After only two weeks on the job and hundreds of frustrating hours, I quit. I went home in tears feeling like a failure. I had a bachelor's degree, no job, and no vision for my life, but this was when God's plan began to unfold. Hallelujah! I went from unemployed to teaching at a modeling school and becoming one of the most sought-after modeling instructors with that company. It was so funny to me because the absolute last thing I ever wanted to do in life was teach, but it was in God's plan all along. From there, the doors to work as a full-time high school teacher opened up, and the opportunity to become a television host came.

During the most difficult time in my life, God began to display His unconditional love for me and, in turn, laid out the plans for my future. What could have really taken me deeper into depression was used to usher me into the most impressionable time of my life. From the death of my father to the beginnings of *Masterpieces Consulting Solutions Inc.*, I was able to make a positive difference in the lives of thousands of people. I never knew that the experiences of my life were going to be the testimonies I would need to encourage students and adults alike. As a host on a television show on the Trinity Broadcasting Network, there was never a guest on the show that I interviewed that I did not have a personal story to contribute. It made me laugh after each episode when I would look at how God allowed even the most insignificant experiences of my life to contribute to the smooth flow of an interview segment. I can recall one guest on the show discussing home-owner safety and the prevention of household toxin exposure.

During a particular episode, one particular guest was not very verbose, which meant that I had more time than questions. Because God allowed me to be a home-owner and ironically, I had used paint stored in my home's utility closet, I was able to interject questions about my own inquisitions about keeping them inside or outside of the home. At the time, this tiny aspect of my life was vital to the success of this segment. Had God not allowed me to purchase my home and have the previous owners leave paint cans inside of the home, eight years later, I may not have had much to say during this interview. Hilarious yet meaningful. When you realize who God truly is, how He feels about you, and how His love heals, loving others comes naturally. Remind yourself that God loves you and then, in turn, love others. People need more positive and optimistic influences in their lives. You are one of them.

Chapter Three Reflections:

1. Your story matters! (1 Cor. 3:7; 1 John 5:4). Recall an experience in your life that can help someone else.

_____

_____

_____

_____

2. Helping others benefits you. (Revelations 12:11) How can you demonstrate compassion towards someone else?

_____

_____

_____

_____

3. Be intentional with being positive. (Ps. 118:6) What steps can you take today that can frame positive behaviors during your daily routines?

_____

_____

___

___

4. Receive the unconditional love of God (Eph. 2:4-6). In what ways have you experienced God's unconditional love in action?

___

___

___

5. Don't despise the small opportunities to do good to others (Job 8:7). Identify 5 "Acts of Kindness" you can display in your home, community, workplace, neighborhood, etc.

___

___

___

___

CHAPTER 4:

Earnestly Convey Excellence

"I in them, and You in Me; in order that they may become one and perfectly united, that the world may know and definitely recognize that You sent Me and that You have loved them even as You love Me."

John 17:23 (Amp.)

My Life

I would consider myself the perfect "imperfectionist." As much as I try to be perfect, I am constantly proving that I simply am not. Can you relate? It is a known fact that there is no perfect person on this earth, no matter how close someone may have appeared to come to it. I mean, I didn't mean to disappoint you. Most people want to be right and want to do their very best in all things, but then, there are those who really do not care.

I can recall countless times when I was a high school teacher that my students would haphazardly complete an assignment. Often times, the assignment didn't even have a name on it. I can recall this one particular time when the students were given the assignment to write a paper on a vocation of their choice. It was to be something of interest to them, and they had to have at least three references to support their topic. Well, one student decided he just didn't have enough time to complete the assignment as expected. Being the innovative and resourceful person that he was, he decided to just find a few websites and pamphlets to copy his information from and use them to construct his paper. Let me be clear, he literally copied the entire pamphlet and turned it in as his paper, no personal thought or contribution of his own at all. But he did put his name on the paper. Now, I was his teacher for almost an entire school year, and knowing his level of vocabulary, I knew immediately that he did not write that paper, none of it. When I questioned him about the paper, he was furious. He denied having copied it. I told him to be honest and that if he were honest, he would have an opportunity to rewrite it for partial credit. He continued to lie. I, of course, had to call his mother and tell her about the situation.

I expected that she would be extremely disappointed and would support my decision for his ability to rectify the issue. To my surprise and utter disbelief, the parent did not agree with my decision and even said she knew he wrote the paper because she helped him! She came to the school unannounced to confront me about the situation. She became so unruly that the police had to be called. I was petrified. No, not so much because the cops were called or even because of the paper, but because of the lengths this parent went to in order to support her child's wrongdoings. Oh, I failed to mention earlier, this was at a Christian academy! We, the believers in Christ, the true representatives of God "should" know better. Not just know better, but want better and should consistently strive to be a good example for others to see, especially the younger generation. So many have a "take it" or "leave it" attitude and this not only grieves God, but limits the abundant life Jesus died for us to have. *"The thief cometh not but for to steal and to kill and to destroy, but I have come that they might have life and that they may have it more abundantly"* John 10:10.

Our willingness to operate in excellence serves two purposes. One, it connects us to the family of God. It's like a good hotel chain. Because that hotel chain has a good rating system and you have stayed at multiple locations, you trust that at any time you make a reservation to stay there, it will be pleasant. Because of their reputation and standards, you would easily recommend that hotel to another person because you have confidence in the overall quality of service that hotel provides. In like manner, if the experience is horrible, you would never stay there nor recommend it to another person. We are like that. When we choose to earnestly convey excellence, we are sending a message and creating a brand for our character. This "brand" of ours enables us to be trusted and recommended. Perfection and excellence are what we strive for, but we must be willing to put in the effort to be and do our very best in all we do.

A Perfect God

God is the only perfect being in creation. Jesus, the Son of God, was tempted in all ways, yet He was without sin. Now, God knows that we are not perfect. That is why God sent His son Jesus to die for us. He knew that we were born with a sinful nature because of the fall of man. He knew that by nature, we would make mistakes over and over again. He knew we would need a way to get to the Father and be redeemed. Thank you, Lord! In retrospect, God wants us to earnestly, with all our hearts, convey excellence. That is what Jesus did, and if we are joint heirs with Him, we need to represent Him in the same way. Oh, I hear the irritation in your mind. This is not possible to do! We are all doomed to err and make mistakes! This is so true.

On several occasions, Jesus speaks of the importance of abiding in Him: *"If ye abide in me, and my words abide in you, ye shall ask what ye will, and it shall be done unto you"* (John 15:7). *"Abide in me, and I in you. As the branch cannot bear fruit of itself, except it abide in the vine; no more can ye except ye abide in me"* (John 15:4). *"If a man abide not in me, he is cast forth as a branch, and is withered; and men gather them, and cast them into the fire, and they are burned"* (John 15:6). We are equipped to perform in excellence when we lean on and depend on God DAILY. It is amazing that when we get help or ask questions, we have a better result. Like many, I had to learn to humble myself and ask for help in order to produce a good product. It is not absurd nor a sign of weakness to ask for help when you are unable to produce in excellence, but you have to ask. Excellence requires wise counsel and insight. Remember, no one besides Jesus Christ Himself was perfect. So being diligent about seeking out knowledge and methods that will guide you in the direction of excellence is best. That's what we call EXCELLENCE!

God's Masterpiece

My pursuit for excellence led me to obtain a master's degree. This was always a goal of mine. However, I was uncertain of which degree to pursue. At one time, I had aspirations of being a model, a pediatrician, a child psychologist, and a television news anchor. When I was attending college as an undergraduate student, I knew moving was ultimately required to become a news reporter and at the time that was something I was not willing to do. Big mistake, I later thought! So, I changed my degree to Public Relations. This degree was still in the area of communications and would enable me to work for myself, which was my ultimate goal. As life, I mean, God would have it, I went on to become a teacher following my recruitment of students for a fashion show. All I could do was yield and just accept the path that God was placing me on.

During this time as a teacher at the school, I discovered what type of master's degree I wanted to pursue. Now, this discovery was followed by an experience I had with one of my students. While teaching at a high school, I taught a senior speech class. I, the girl who was terrified to speak in front of others, was teaching a speech class. I recall one of my students, in particular, who was considered one of the best female basketball players in Florida. She was so cute but so shy. Of course, the students would have to stand in front of their peers and present a speech in the class. She progressively did better and better and passed the course. When the semester had ended, I remember like it was yesterday, how she looked, sounded, and felt about the course.

With humility in her voice, she said to me, "Ms. Taylor, thank you for helping me talk in front of people. You changed my life." Of course, my entire day was enlightened, and tears most definitely were shed because I could recall the times when I was deathly afraid to speak in front of a group of people. I never could have imagined God would use me to help someone else overcome that fear. (SN: It is a known fact that people would rather die than to give a eulogy at a funeral.) This young lady had no idea that her mere acknowledgment of my helping her set the path for my quest in obtaining my master's degree and becoming a speech-language pathologist. You see, my desire has always been to please God. In pleasing God, I can confidently expect circumstances to turn out all right. Psalms 37: 4 says, *"Delight thyself also in the Lord, and He will give thee the desires of thine heart."*

I don't know about you, but it brings me such comfort and relief to know that asking for help and relying on God is not only encouraging but a MUST! As God's masterpiece, we don't always know how the pieces of the puzzle will come together. All we have is a picture in mind of what it may look like. But, God, the master craftsman, the potter, and carpenter, already knows exactly what the outcome will be. We can find so many references in the Bible that clarify God's complete desire and intention to mold us into what He has already ordained for us to be. Take a look:

"But now, O Lord, thou art our father; we are the clay, and thou our potter; and **we all are the work of thy hand** *."* Isaiah 64:8 (KJV)

"O house of Israel, cannot I do with you as this potter saith the Lord. Behold, as the clay is in the potter's hand, **so are ye in mine hand***, O house of Israel."* Jeremiah 18:6 (KJV)

"*And the vessel that he made of clay was marred in the hand of the potter;* **so he made it again another vessel**, *as seemed good to the potter to make it.*" Jeremiah 18:4

"*Surely your turning of things upside down shall be esteemed as the potter's clay; for shall the work say of him that made it, He made me not or shall the thing framed say of him that framed it, He had no understanding?*" Isaiah 29:16 (KJV)

    We cannot tell ourselves how we should function and how we should perform. Only the creator of a thing can do that. Even though we may not understand the crushing and breaking when we are in a process of life, God has a purpose for each line, crack, and fracture. Acknowledging the beauty in the mess and the necessity of chaos or frustration that God allows are empowering. Not only is it empowering, but it's also freeing! Our dependence on God propels us into purpose. I can't even begin to share all of the times I looked up to heaven and asked God why would he let me go through this, AGAIN!

Mother-Daughter Relationship

One of the most important ways that I wanted to demonstrate excellence in love was in my relationship with my mother. As the only girl of three (3) brothers, I often had to find my place amongst my siblings. My being a tomboy and a daddy's girl were two ways that I attempted to solidify my identity, but that did not work. My relationship with my mom was important too. Although very different in ways, I vied for the attention of my mother. As a little girl, I would write my mother love letters every day and make her little gifts to win her affection. But her affection was something I already had; I just didn't know it.

Throughout my childhood, we had our challenges, which were not easy. As I grew into a young lady and then an adult, I began to recognize that my ability to trust others with my emotions and my heart was tainted. I would quickly get offended or overly sensitive to what others would say about me because I lacked a true love for myself and the right self- identity. It was extremely toxic and draining. One day, an argument that could have completely severed my relationship with my mother erupted during what I would have considered one of the most pivotal times in my life. This, of course, added to this turbulent moment.

You see, this masterpiece was crumbling and spinning out of control. For the first time ever, I did not spend the holidays with my family. I spent it crying on my couch, watching Christmas movies alone. It was horrible, literally the lowest of lows. Looking back now, I realized this breakdown was necessary. Sometimes God has to completely demolish what was seemingly standing to establish a more secure and firm foundation so that He can make our relationships and our identities into what He originally purposed. I had to let go of the past and give up the hope for a better past. This and many other moments were mere outbreaks of suppressed hurt and pain.

Let's be honest: we do not attend to our inner feelings and emotions like we should. We carry on as broken people on the inside while looking whole on the outside. I had to do something about it. I knew I could not continue living that way. I wanted a change. I wanted to enjoy each day of my life and live a long life. So, my mother and I went to therapy, and, yeah, it was rough at the beginning, very rough. We spoke to the therapist and not one another. We were eventually forced to speak and even take outings together. I know this sounds sad, but the ending was beautiful. Slowly but surely, we began the building of a new relationship. We both had to commit to complete honesty about our feelings for one another and not put on "the face" for the sake of the other. Although the process was hard, it has been totally worth it.

The greatest part about all of this is the fact that all my other relationships have benefitted from this process as well. Excellence takes work and intentionality. However, when it comes to people, honestly, it's not all easy, and sometimes it is not even possible. *"Do all that you can to live in peace with everyone"* ***Romans 12:18 (NLT).*** This verse allows us to see that we must do our part, which is the only part that we can control. We cannot control the part of peace concerning other people. There's a saying I've been hearing lately: "what you think about me is none of my business." In other words, I should not be overly consumed with what someone else thinks about me. I should be more concerned about what my thoughts are towards the other.

Hebrews 12:14 (NLT)

"Work at living in peace with everyone, and work at living a holy life, for those who are not holy will not see the Lord."

I John 4:18 (KJV)

"There is no fear in love; but perfect love casteth out fear; because fear hath torment. He that feareth is not made perfect in love."

God has given us instructions pertaining to how we should think and conduct ourselves. Can you recall a time when you did not put forth your best effort? Maybe a time when you were asked to bake cookies for a bake sale, yet you opted to just purchase store-bought cookies instead? And then you lied about baking them? Tisk! Tisk! Our desires should be to do things with honesty, integrity, and credibility. Compromising right for wrong is a form of settling and can result in a life of mediocrity. God is calling us higher and expects us to complete His assignments in excellence. There is no Plan B for the world. God's church, the people of God, is all we have.

I had so many opportunities to give up and not do my best while in graduate school. On many occasions, I was tempted to cheat on exams or submit someone else's paper as mine. Yes!!! I was tempted. The program was so difficult and required so much hard work, sacrifice, and rigor; many times, I did not think I would finish. I mean, I was really beginning to think that I was just a hamster on its wheel spinning in never-ending circles. It was tumultuous! The beauty in it all was that I learned how to push through the discomfort and the pain, knowing that the price I was paying would be worth it at the end.

> *"For I press toward the mark for the prize of the high calling of God in Christ Jesus." Philippians 3:14*

It is time for us to press towards the mark of excellence. We can practice this excellence in love, on our jobs, in our relationship with God, and our relationships with people. As I continue to grow as an adult woman, I realize more and more the importance of doing things the right way the first time. Now, don't get me wrong, at times, the shortcut often is appealing, and yes, I take it. But in the end, it costs more than what we should have paid. For example, in graduate school, I had to write many, many research papers, and we had to include sources. Well, on more than one occasion, I would think to just write my paper first and then add my sources later. Not such a smart move. This was not a smart choice because, in most cases, I would have to change my pre-written paper. After all, the evidence did not support my thesis, or I would learn something new and find it more interesting than what I had already written. Big waste of time. So, in those moments, I learned to not always look for shortcuts, but the best method that demonstrates excellence in my prospective task. Colossians 3:23 reminds us to: *"Work willingly at whatever you do, as though you were working for the Lord rather than for people."*

God simply wants us to operate in the capacity that He has given us when He asks us to do something. Everything should be done as unto the Lord so that the world will know that we are His children. You have to remember that we are going to have to give an account for everything we do here on earth. Knowing this, we should want to do as God commands, and that is to walk in excellence. "For we are God's masterpiece. He has created us anew in Christ Jesus, so we can do the good things he planned for us long ago." (NLT)

Chapter Four Reflections:

1. You are a work in progress (Matthew 5:48). What areas in your life would you say needs some work?

_____
_____
_____
_____

2. You are worth the ultimate prize (Philippians 3:14). Do you believe that you are deserving of God's best? Why or why not?

_____
_____
_____
_____

3. Your work ethic is important to God (Colossians 3:23). How can you better demonstrate excellence in the workplace?

_____
_____

_____

_____

4. You are equipped to do your part on earth (Romans 12:18). What gifts and talents enable you to fulfill God's purpose for your life?

_____

_____

_____

_____

5. Accepting that you are a masterpiece is the ultimate acceptance of love (Ephesians 2:10). How can you remind yourself each day that you are a masterpiece?

_____

_____

_____

_____

Conclusion

For we are made accurately suited to exemplify righteousness; be a positive influence while earnestly conveying excellence. It is evident that the principles written in this book are impossible to manifest without the Holy Spirit. Philippians 4:13 declares, *"I can do all things through Christ who strengthens me."* The key phrase in this verse is "through Christ." It's as if you are in a cocoon, and you are becoming a beautiful butterfly. Christ is the cocoon, and you are the butterfly being nourished, protected, and strengthened each and every day. When we don't experience this assistance, we are helpless and incomplete. He completes us and enables us to fulfill every aspect of our lives. In many ways, this is a relief because we can rest in God knowing that God is doing the work.

Our heavenly Father loves us and is in love with you. There are endless possibilities when we allow God to unveil the masterpiece within us all. You have what it takes: make the choice today to be God's masterpiece. Hey, nobody can do what you can do like you can do it! And when in doubt, ask yourself this question, "If I tried to be like someone else, who would be me?"

Now What?

I shared these stories with you to show you just how much God loves us and is ultimately in control of our lives as long as we stay in His will. On our journey and while we operate in our purpose, we may face hard times. When I was completing my master's degree in speech-language pathology, I faced many medical issues that landed me in the hospital. I was forced to quit a job with nothing lined up. My yearly income was less than $10,000 per year. My car continued to breakdown, and I had my lion's share of anxiety, disagreeable professors, unreasonable supervisors, familial crises, and oh, let us not forget depression, oppression, loneliness, and fear. Yet, through it all, I was able to graduate with Honors.

Ending Line

When we stop and realize that the circumstances in our lives come to push us forward, we can then accept the truth that what appeared to be broken in our lives were simply pieces of our life's puzzle. This is how we become God's Masterpiece.

"You, therefore, must be perfect [growing into complete maturity of godliness in mind and character, having reached the proper height of virtue and integrity], as your heavenly Father is perfect." Matthew 5:48 Amp

About Michellita

Michellita Taylor, M.S, CCC-SLP is a native of Jacksonville, Florida and is a licensed speech-language pathologist. She received her bachelor's degree from the University of North Florida and her graduate degree with honors from Nova Southeastern University. Michellita is also a professional model, an accomplished singer, television host, instructor, and business owner of Masterpieces Consulting Solutions Inc.

Her education and experience in the field of communications have created a solid platform for her broadcast journalism and public speaking career that began fifteen years ago. Michellita has hosted TBN's "Joy in Our Town" television show and has made appearances on Channel 12's First Coast Living as the "Etiquette Expert."

In addition to having the gift of speaking, her melodic voice and a passion for worship have afforded her the opportunity to sing on various platforms, including her church's worship team at Celebration Church in Jacksonville, Florida. Michellita has traveled the globe and shared the stage with numerous highly esteemed artists such as Reba McIntyre, Marvin Sapp, Israel Houghton, Donnie McClurkin, and CeCe Winans. She was also privileged to sing and grace the stage in Lugano, Switzerland, during the annual Blues to Bop Music Festival.

Michellita has acquired many opportunities to display her beauty and grace in various pageants, fashion shows, and local as well as national magazine publications. Her desire to represent Christ by way of modeling and her mission to change the degrading images portrayed by media today encouraged her to start her own business, Masterpieces Consulting Solutions Inc., which is a consulting group that provides consultation in modeling, etiquette, and professional development for individuals and businesses.

Michellita's passion for transforming lives has allowed her to be a trailblazer in northeast Florida and around the world. Being the victim of bullying as a little girl, Michellita suffered from low self-esteem and lacked a true positive identity. She found confidence and strength by competing in pageants. Drawing upon her past pageant experiences as a contestant, titleholder, and director for over 15 years enabled Michellita to take the plunge and launch the Miss Charisma Scholarship Pageant seven years ago. Michellita has since been able to personally mentor and train over 150 girls! Her life's motto is, "We are God's masterpieces created with everything we need to fulfill our life's purpose on this planet."

www.ingramcontent.com/pod-product-compliance
Lightning Source LLC
Chambersburg PA
CBHW072104110526
44590CB00018B/3306